SCHOLARLY RESOURCES, INC.
Wilmington, Delaware • London

Reprint edition published in 1975

Library of Congress Catalog Card Number: 75-3692
ISBN: 0-8420-1883-2

Manufactured in the United States of America

ACTS AND RESOLUTIONS

OF THE

GENERAL COUNCIL

OF THE

Choctaw Nation

Passed at Its Regular Session, 1901

HERALD PRESS, CADDO.

1902.

Acts of the Choctaw Nation

BILL NO. 1

Be it resolved by the General Council of the Choctaw Nation assembled:

That the chairman of the Finance Committee shall appoint a clerk for the said committee, whose duty it shall be to make and keep a full record of the work of said committee.

Be it further resolved: That the clerk of the said Finance Committee shall receive for his services five dollars ($5.00) per day. That the National Auditor shall issue his warrant for actual services, and the Treasurer shall pay the same. And this resolution shali take effect and be in force from and after its passage and approval.

S. E. LEWIS.

Approved, Oct. 9, 1901

G. W. DUKES,
Principal Chief, C. N.

BILL NO. 2

A RESOLUTION Creating clerk for Committee on Petitions for October term, 1901.

Be it resolved by the General Council of the Choctaw Nation assembled :

SEC. 1. That the Chairman of the Committee on Petitions shall appoint a clerk for the said Committee, whose duty it shall be to make and keep a full record of the work of said Committee.

SEC. 2. *Be it further resolved:* That the clerk of the said Committee on Petitions shall receive for his services four dollars ($4.00) per day; that the National Auditor shall issue his warrant for actual services, and the Treasurer shall pay the same. And this resolution shall take effect and be in force from and after its passage and approval.

S. E. LEWIS.

Approved Oct., 12, 1901

G. W. DUKES,
Principal Chief, C. N.

BILL NO. 3.

A RESOLUTION Creating clerk for School Committee:

Be it resolved by the General Council of the Choctaw Nation assembled:

That the Chairman of the School Committee shall appoint a clerk for said Committee whose duty it shall be to make and keep a full record of all work of said Committee.

Be it further resolved: That the clerk of the School Committee shall receive for his services four dollars ($4.00) per day; that the National Auditor shall issue his warrant for actual services and the Treasurer shall pay the same. And that this resolution shall take effect and be in force from and after its passage.

W. C. WARD.

Approved Oct., 11th, 1901.

G. W. DUKES,
Principal Chief, C. N.

BILL NO. 4.

A RESOLUTION Creating clerk for Committee on Chiefs Message:

Be it resolved by the General Council of the Choctaw Nation assembled:

SEC. 1. That the Chairman of the Committee on on Chiefs Message shall appoint a clerk for said Committee whose duty it shall be to make and keep a full record of the work of said committee.

SEC. 2. *Be it further rasolved*: That the Clerk of the said Committee on Chiefs Message shall receive for his services the sum of four dollars ($4.00) per day, that the National Auditor shall issue his warrant for actual services and the Treasurer shall pay the same, and this resolution shall take effect and be in force from and after its passage and approval

J. C. FOLSOM.

Approved, Oct., 12, 1901

G. W. DUKES,
Principal Chief, C. N.

BILL NO. 5.

AN ACT Changing an election precinct in Wade County.

Be it resolved by the General Council of the Choctaw Nation assembled:

That the election precinct in Wade County, known as Pleasant Hill Precinct, be and the same is hereby removed and located at Wadesville School House, one mile East, and to be called and known as Wadesville Election Precinct; and all future elections shall be held there; and this act shall take effect and be in force from and after its passage.

L. D. VAUGHN

Approved Oct., 10, 1901.

G. W. DUKES,
Principal Chief, C. N.

BILL NO. 6.

A RESOLUTION Accepting the report of Amos Henry, showing the disbursements made by him out of the contingent fund allowed him as School Trustee of the First District.

Your committee, to whom was referred the report of Amos Henry, School Trustee of the First District, giving an itemized account of the expecditures made by him out of his contingent fund of $75.00 from November, 1900, to and including September 1901, have carefully examined the report and find that he has expended one dollar ($1.00) in excess of his allowance, but that all his expenditures were made in the discharge of his official duties. Your committee would, therefore recommend the adoption of the following resolution:

Be it resolved by the General Council of the Choctaw Nation assembled:

SEC. 1. That the Report of Amos Henry School Trustee of the First District, showing the expenditures made by him out of his contingent fund for November, 1900, to and and including September, 1901, be, and the same is hereby accepted as true and correct.

SEC. 2. That this resolution shall take effect and be in force from and after its passage and approval.

GREEN MCCURTAIN
Chairman Finance Committee.

BILL NO. 8.

AN ACT Creating a commission to negotiate an agreement with the Commission to the Five Civilized Tribes to close the citizenship rolls, and for the settlement of all other matters.

Not returned from the President.

BILL NO. 7.

A RESOLUTION Accepting the report of George W. Scott, National Treasurer, giving an itemized account of the expenditures made by him out of the contingent fund of the Treasury of the Choctaw Nation.

Your committee to whom was referred the report of George W. Scott, National Treasurer, giving an itemized account of the expenditures made by him out of the contingent fund of the Treasury of the Choctaw Nation during the years of 1900 and 1901, have carefully examined the report and find that all disbursements were made by him in the discharge of his official duties and in furnishing the National Treasurer's office with necessary supplies and fixtures. On September 30, 1901, there was a balance on hand of $107.78, which amount was refunded to the Treasury of the Choctaw Nation, as shown by his annual report. Your committee would therefore, recommend the adoption of the following resolution:

Be it resolved by the General Council of the Choctaw Nation assembled

SEC. 1 That the report of George W. Scott, National Treasurer, showing the expenditures made by him out of the contingent fund of the Treasury of the Choctaw Nation during the years of 1900 and 1901, be, and the same is hereby accepted as true and correct.

SEC. 2. That this resolution shall take effect and be in force from and after its passage and approval.

GREEN MCCURTAIN,
Chairman of Finance Committee.

Approved Oct. 15th, 1901.

G. W. DUKES,
Principal Chief, C. N.

BILL No. 9.

AN ACT Changing an election precinct in Gaines County.

Be it enacted by the General Council of the Choctaw Nation assembled:

That the election precinct in Gaines County known as

Hartshorne Precinct, be and the same is hereby removed and located at Mountain Station, eight miles southeast, and to be called and known as Mountain Station Election Precinct; and all future elections shall be held there; and this act shall take effect and be in force from and after its passage and approval.

JACKSON JONES,

Approved Oct., 22, 1901.

G. W. DUKES,
Principal Chief, C. N.

BILL NO. 10.

WHEREAS, we have heard with sorrow of the recent death of several of our fellow-citizens, namely.

W. N. Jones, ex-Principal Chief of the Choctaw Nation, who died June 11, 1901;

J. W. Everidge, Judge of the Supreme Court of the Choctaw Nation, who died May 5, 1901;

R. M. Jones an ex-Member of Council from Atoka County who died September 22, 1901;

Stephen Roberts, several times a representative of Atoka County, who died during July, 1901;

H. C. Harris, Judge of the Supreme Court of the Choctaw Nation, who died ....;

Robert Kanimubbee, Senator for ten years, representing Nashoba and Eagle Counties, who died March 5, 1901;

Daniel Hudson, a Representative of Eagle County for several years, who died June 9, 1901;

Isham Goings, a Representative of Eagle County for several years, who died during May, 1901:

Charles Winston, Member of of Council from Towson County, who died December 1900; and,

WHEREAS, we recall with pride their zealous devotion to the interests of their people; and,

WHEREAS, it is fitting and proper that we should pause in our labors to pay a tribute of respect to the meanory of those who in positions of honor and trust, faithfully served their country long and well; Now therefore,

Be it resolved by the General Council of the Choctaw Nation assembled:

SEC. 1. That we extend our sincere condolence to the families of the deceased;

SEC. 2. *Be it further resolved,* That as a token of respect to the memory of the deceased the General Council do adjourn Wednesday next, October, 16, at 12 o'clock a. m. until the following Monday.

SEC. 3. *Be it further resolved,* That these resolutions be entered upon the journal of both houses of the General Council, and that the National Secretary be, and he is hereby, required to furnish a copy of the same to the family of each of the deceased.

GREEN MCCURTAIN

Approved Oct., 14th, 1901. G. W. DUKES,

Principal Chief, C. N.

BILL NO. 11.

A RESOLUTION Declining the petition of Willie Jones.

We your committee to whom was referred the petition of Willie Jones for the pay of $760.00 claimed by him as damages incurred, have carefully examined said claim and found that said claim is not justly due to the said Willie Jones, and would therefore recommend the adoption of the following resolution:

Be it resolved by the General Council of the Choctaw Nation assembled:

That the petition of Willie Jones for seven hundred and sixty dollars ($760.00) as claimed herein, the same is hereby rejected, and that this resolution shall take effect and be in force from and after its passage and approval.

S. E. LEWIS,

Chairman Committee on Petitions.

Approved Oct. 23, 1901. G. W. DUKES,

Principal Chief, C. N.

BILL NO. 12.

A RESOLUTION Declining the petition of Isham Walker.

We your committee to whom was referred the petition of Isam Walker for the payment of $365.00 claimed as District Attorney fees, have carefully considered said petition and are of the opinion that said claim is not justly due, and would therefore recommend the adoption of the following resolution.

Be it resolved by the General Council of the Choctaw Nation assembled:

That the petition of Isham Walker for three hnndred and sixty five dollars claim for attorney fee be and the same is hereby denied, and that this resolution shall take effect and be in force from and after its passage and approval;

S. E. LEWIS,
Chm. Com. on Petitions.

Approved Oct. 23, 1901:

G. W. DUKES,
Principal Chief, C. N.

BILL NO. 13.

A RESOLUTION Accepting the report of T. E. Sanguin, Collector for the Third District of the Choctaw Nation, for the quarters ended December 31, 1900, March 31, 1901, and June 30, 1901.

Your committee to whom was referred the report of T. E. Sanguin, Collector for the thlrd district of the Choctaw Nation, reporting amounts collected by him from licensed traders in his district, have carefully examined the report and find that it covers the quarters ended December 31, 1900 March 31, 1901, June 30, 1901, and shows that the total amount due the Choctaw Nation is $10,603.21,. Our examination of the report showed that the total amount actually due is $10,606.81, or a shortage of $3.60.

We were furnished receipts, signed by the National Treasurer, showing the payment by Mr. Sanguin into the National Treasury of the total amount due according to his report, or $10.603.21; we were also furnished satisfatory evidence of the payment by him into the National Treasury of the amount of the shortage, or $3.60.

Your commiteee, would, therefore, recommend the adoption of the following resolution.

Be it resolved by the General Council of the Choctrw Nation assembled:

SEC. 1. That the report of T. E. Sanguin, Collector for the Third District of the Choctaw Nation, be, and the same is hereby, accepted as true and correct.

SEC. 2. That this resolution shall take effect and be in force from and after its passage and approval,

GREEN MCCURTAIN
Chm Finance Com.

Approved Oct., 23, 1901.

G. W. DUKES,
Principal Chief, C. N

BILL NO. 14.

A RESOLUTION Asking for the relief of Mother M. Virginia.

Disapproved by the President, Dec.,12, 1901.

BILL NO. 15.

A RESOLUTION Accepting the report of Jeff Fulton, showing expenditures made out of the contingent fund allowed him as School Trustee for the Third District of the of the Choctaw Nation.

Your committee to whom was referred the report of Jeff Fulton, School Trustee for the Third District of the Choctaw Nation, giving an itemized account of the expenditures made by him out of his contingent fund of $75.00, from March 18, 1901, to and including May 28, 1901, have carefully examined report and fine that the total amount expended by him in the discharge of his official duties was $72.20. To this amount Mr. Fulton added the discount at which he sold his national warrant. The discount was 15 per centum, or $11.25, making the total amount reported by him as having been expended $83.45.

Your commlttee believes that National officers should not be allowed a credit for the discount at which they may dispose of the warrants paid them as salaries or allowed them as contingent expenses. Your committee further believes that the difference between Mr. Fulton's contingent fund and the amount expended by him in the discharge of his official duties, or $2.80, should be refunded to the National Treasury.

We would threfore recommend the adoption of the following resolution:

Be it resolved by the General Council of the Choctaw Nation assembled:

SEC. 1. That the report of Jeff Fulton, School Trustee for the Third Distrlct of the Choctaw Nation, showing the expenditures made by him out of his contingent fund of $75.00, be, and the same is hereby, accepted as true and correct so far as it shows amounts expended by him in the discharge of his official duties, or to the amount of $72,20

SEC. 2. That the National Treasurer is hereby authorized and directed to make demand on Mr. Fulton for the balance of his contingent fund now on hand, or $2.80, and to report to the next General council the result of his actions under this resolution.

SEC. 3. That this resolution shall take effect and be in force from and after its passage and approval,

GREEN MCCURTAIN,
Chm. Finance Com.

Approved Oct.. 29th 1901.

G. W. DUKES,
Principal Chief, C. N.

BILL NO. 16.

A RESOLUTION Accepting the report of C. J. Anderson showing expenditures made out of the contingent fund allowed him as School Trustee for the Second District of the Choctaw Nation.

Your committee to whom was referred the report of C.

J. Anderson, School Trustee for the Second District of the Choctaw Nation, giving an itemized account of the expenditures made by him out of his contingent fund of $75.00 during the fiscal year ended September, 30, 1901, have carefully examined the report and find that the total amount expended by him in the discharge of his official duties was $54.25. To this amount Mr. Anderson added the discount at which he sold his national warrant. The Discount was 20 per centum, or $15.00, making the total amount reported by him as having been expended $69.25.

Your committee believes that the National officers should not be allowed a credit for the discount at which they may dispose of the warrants paid them as salaries or allowed them as contingent expenses. Your committee further believes that the difference between Mr. Anderson's contingent fund and the amount expended by him in the discharge of his official duties, or $20.75, should be refunded to the National Treasury.

We would, therefore, recommend the adoption of the following resolution:

Be it resolved by the General Council of the Choctaw Nation assembled:

SEC; 1. That the report of C. J. Anderson School Trustee for the Second District of the Choctaw Nation, showing the amounts expended by him out of his contingent fund of $75.00, be and the same is hereby, accepted as true and correct so far as it shows amount expended by him in the disbharge of his official duties, or to the amount of $54.25.

SEC. 2. That the National Treasurer is hereby authorized and directed to make demand on Mr. Crawford for the balance of his contingent fund now on hand, or $20.75, and to report to the next General Council the result of his actions under this resolution.

SEC. 3. That this resolution shall take effect and be in force from and after its passage and approval.

GREEN MCCURTAIN,
Chm. Finance Com.

Approved Oct., 29, 1901.

G. W. DUKES,
Principal Chief C. N.

BILL No. 17.

A RESOLUTION accepting the annual report of William Bryant, Collector for the Second District of the Choctaw Nation.

Your committee two whom was referred the annual report of William Bryant, Collector for the Second District of the Choctaw Nation, have carefully examined the report and find that it covers the quarters ended December 31, 1900, March 31, 1901, June 30, 1901, and September 30, 1901, and shows that the total amount due the Choctaw Nation is $363.27. Our examination of the report shows that the total amount actually due is $361.62, making an over-payment by Mr, Bryant of $1;65. which amount we have refunded to him.

We were furnished satisfactory evidence of the payment by Mr. Bryant into the National Treasury of the amount due the nation according to our examination of his report. Attention is called to the fact however, that among the national warrants submitted by Mr Bryant in payment of the above amount were two school warrants, described as follows:

No. 10, for $20.00 issued by C, J. Anderson, Trustee of the Second district, dated February 23, 1900 and payable to L. S. Bohanan, for services rendered as teacher of the Spring Hill Neighborhood School in Nashoba County, from January 1, 1900, to and including January 26, 1900.

No. 15, for $12.00 issued by C. J. Anderson, Trustee of the Second District, dated March 9, 1900, and payable to D. S. Noah, for services rendered as teacher of the Albion neighborhood school in Wade County, from January, 30, 1900, to and including February 26, 1900.

An examination of these warrants by your committee shows that they were issued under an act passed by the General Council at the regular session of October, 1899. wherein the School Board of the Choctaw Nation was authorized to continue our schools and to issue warrants in payment of school expenses.

Inasmuch as these warrants were legally issued, your

committee has directed the National Treasurer to receive them from Mr Bryant in payment of the amount due the nation by him. Your committee would therefore recommend the adoption of the following resolution:

Be it resolved by the General Council of the Choctaw Nation assembled

SEC. 1. That the annual report of William Bryant, Collector for the Second District of of the Choctaw Nation be and the same is hereby accepted as true and eorrect.

SEC. 2. That this resolution shall take effect and be in force from and after its passage and approval.

GREEN MCCURTAIN,
Chairman of Finance Committee.

Approved Oct. 30th, 1901.

G. W. DUKES,
Principal Chief, C. N.

BILL NO. 18.

AN ACT For the relief of J. A. Williams.

Whereas, during the scholastic year of 1899 and 1900 while the school affairs of the Choctaw Nation were in an unsettled condition and it was unknow whether the schools of the Nation were to be conducted under the supervision of the Interior Department of the United States, or of the tribal authorities, one J. A. Williams did teach a neighborhood school of Choctaw pupils under the authority and recommendation of the Choctaw Board of Education and, whereas,

The said J. A. Williams under said authority taught for the period of five months for which he has never received any compensation and whereas, recognizing the claim of J. A. Williams is just and correct and that he is entitled to the sum of one hundred and forty-three dollars and eighty cents ($143.80,) for services as teacher rendered to the Choctaw Nation, therefore;

Be it enacted by the General Council of the Choctaw Nation assembled:

SEC. 1. That the Honorable Secretary of the Interior is hereby respectfully requested and thereto authorized to pay the said J. A. Williams the sum of one hundred and forty-three dollars and eighty cents ($143.80) for and in behalf of the Choctaw Nation out of the school funds of said nation now to the credit of said nation in the Sub-treasury of the United States, for services rendered as teacher as shown by the following school report; to-wit

Oct. 30, 1899 to Nov. 24, 1899,.........20 days.........$30.10
Nov. 27, 1899 to Dec. 22, 1899,.........20 days.........$29.50
Jan. 1st. 1900 to Jan. 26, 1900,.........20 days.........$29.20
Jan. 29, 1900, to Feb. 23, 1900,.........20 days.........$29.00
Feb. 26, 1900, to Mar. 80, 1900,.........20 days.........$26.00

SEC. 2. *Be it further enacted:* That this act shall take effect and be in force from and aftar its passage and approval

Passed the Senate Oct. 28, 1901. W. G. WARD,
Pres. Pro-tem of the Senate.

Pass the House, Oct. 29, 1901. WM. HARRISON,
Speaker of H. of R.

Approved, Oct., 29, 1901 G. W. DUKES,
Principal Chief, C. N.

White House, Waseineton, D. C., December, 3, 1901.
Approved: T. ROOSEVELT.

BILL NO. 19.

A RESOLUTION of condolence.

Be it resolved by the General Council of the Choctaw Nation assembled:

That we have heard with profound sorrow of the death at the hands of an assassin, of our beloved President William McKinley. He was a man whose life was gentle and kind; his sympathies were always with the masses of his countrymen, and their interests and welfare were his constant study. His public life was above reproach, and his private life typefied all that was best and purest in the American home. He was born in obscurity, yet called by the American people to the highest position in their confidence and love; and, under his wise and patriotic administration of public affairs, new prestige was added to our country and new lustre to our flag.

That the Choctaw people recall with gratitude the many evidences of his friendship for and interest in them, and his efforts to protect them in the enjoyment of all their rights.

That we deplore the fact that he was stricken down by the bloody hand of anarchy while extending friendly greetings to his fellow countrymen.

That we condem anarchy and all the agencies that fosted and encouraged it. We believe that the Uniied States should speedily enact laws that will stamp out anarchy and make its existence forever impossible hereafter in this country.

That we unite with all good citizens in extending our deep sympathy to the bereaved family of our late President.

That these resolutions be entered upon the journal of both houses of the General Council, and that the National Secretary be, and he is hereby, required to furnish a copy of these resolutions to the family of the deceased.

Passed the Senate Oct 12, 1901.

GREEN MCCURTAIN,
President of the Senate.

Passed the House Oct. 12, 1901. WM. HARRISON
Speaker of the H. of R.

Approved Oct. 12, 1901. G. W. DUKES,
Principal Chief. C. N.

BILL NO. 20.

AN ACT Authorizing the sale of Tushkalusa Academy property.

The Committee on Chiefs message to whom was referred the matter of selling Tushkalusa Academy property, have carefully examined the same and respectfully ask the adoption of the following act:

Be it enacted by the General Council of the Choctaw Nation assembled:

SEC. 1. That the Superintendent of Public Instruction

be and he is hereby authorized and directed to sell, after giving thirty (30) days notice in some newspaper published in the Choctaw Nation, at public auction the Tushkalusa Academy property, including buildings, beds furniture and other chattles belonging thereto, for cash in full; and said property shall bring not less than eight hundred dollars ($800.00); and that six hundred dollars of the proceeds of said sale shall be applied to the settlement of Henry Willis Custodian of said property and the said Superintendent of Public instruction is hereby required to demand and accept a receipt of all accounts that the said Henry Willis may now have, or hereafter have against the Choctaw Nation as Custodian of said Academy property and that the balance of the proceeds of the sale shall be placed into the National Treasury for National purposes.

SEC. 2. *Be it further enacted:* That the Superintendent of Public Instruction is hereby authorized to pay for the publication of the notice of this sale out of his contingent fund.

SEC, 3. *Be it further enacted:* That the Superintendent of Public Instruction is empowered to give a bill of sale and good title of said Academy property to the purchaser in the name of the Choctaw Nation, and this act shall take effect and be in force from and after its passage and approval.

Passed the Senate Oct., 29, 1901. JAMES BOWER
Pres. Pro-tem of the Senate

Passed the house Oct. 30, 1901. WM. HARRISON
Speaker of the H. of R.

Approved Oct., 30, 1901. G. W. DUKES,
Principal Chief, C. N.

White House, Washington, D.C., December 3, 1901.
Approved T. ROOSEVELT.

BILL NO. 21.

AN ACT Granting to Frank Lewis a Ferry on Poteau River.

Be it enacted by the General Council of the Choctaw Nation assembled:

SEC. 1. That Frank Lewis a citizen of the Choctaw

Nation is hereby authorized and permitted to establish and operate a ferry-boat on Poteau River in Scullyville County Choctaw Nation, on the road running from Shady-point to Cameron, I. T. at what is known and commonly called "Hay Crossing" or old "Wheeler's Ferry" being one and one-half miles North-east of Shady-point, the said Frank Lewis being the owner of the premises thereat, and this privilege shall continue for the period of four years, and his right herein granted shall extend up and down the said Poteau River for a distance of one mile each way, The said Frank Lewis shall keep the banks and approaches to the ferry boat in good condition, and the Choctaw Nation shall in no wise be responsible or liable to any person for loss or damages by reason of said ferry.

SEC. 2. *Be it further enacted,* That Frank Lewis shall have the right to charge for vehicles, drawn by more than two horses, mules, or oxen, seventy-five cents; for vehicles, drawn by a single animal, thirty cents; for each animal, horse, mule or cattle, ten cents; for each person on horse, twenty-five cents; for each person on foot, ten cents; for each hog or sheep, five cents; for vehicles, drawn by two horses, mules or oxen, fifty cents.

SEC. 3. *Be it further enacted,* That all acts heretofore passed coming in conflict with this act, are hereby repealed, and this act shall take effect and be inforce from and after its passage and approval.

Passed the Senate Oct. 29, 1901. JAMES BOWER,
Pres. Pro-tem Senate

Passed the House, Oct., 30, 1901. WM HARRISON.
Speaker H, of R.

Approved Oct., 30th, 1901. G. W. DUKES,
Principal Chief, C. N.

White House, Washington, D. C., December 2, 1901.
Approved THEODORE ROOSEVELT.

BILL NO. 22.

AN ACT Making an appropriation to pay the American Book Company for books furnished to the Choctaw Nation.

Not returned from the President.

BILL NO. 23.

A RESOLUTION Refusing to accept the statutory allowance of fifty dollars ($50.00) per mile for right of way from the Fort Smith and Western Railway Company through the Choctaw Nation (30 Statute, 1368)

Be it resolved by the General Council of the Choctaw Nation assembled:

That the Choctaw tribe of Indians hereby dissents from the statutory allowance of fifty dollars per mile, Act of Congress March 3rd, 1899 (30 statute 1368) as compensation for said right of way from the Fort Smith & Western Railway Company, and respectfully ask that compensation be determined by arbitration as provided by the specifiic terms of said act of congress, and that this resolution be transmitted to the Secretary of the Interior as evidence of such dissents

Be it further resolved: That this resolution shall take effect and be in force from and after its passage and approval.

J. C. FOLSOM.

Approved Nov., 4th, 1901.

G. W. DUKES,
Principal Chief, C. N.

BILL NO. 24

A RESOLUTION Declining the petition of Thomas Watson.

We your committee to whom was referred the petition of Thomas Watson Ex-Sheriff of Nashoba County, Choctaw Nation for fees claimed for feeding and supporting Soloman Jones a prisoner committed to jail from Wade County Choctaw Nation, have carefully considered the said petition and would recommend that the petition be denied.

Be it resolved by the General Council of the Choctaw Nation assembled:

That the petition of Thomas Watson Ex-Sheriff of Nashoba County Choctaw Nation claiming a fee of $118.85 for feeding and supporting Soloman Jones a prisoner. One hundred and thirty-two days be and the same is hereby denied, and that this resolution shall take effect and be in force from and after its passage and approval.

JOE HOMER,

Approved Nov. 23, 1901. G. W. DUKES,

Principal Chief, C. N.

BILL NO. 25.

A RESOLUTION authorizing the Finance Committee to collect and destroy all canceled Choctaw warrants.

Be it resolved by the General Council of the Choctaw Nation assembled:

SEC. 1. That the Finance Committee is hereby authorized to collect and destroy during the present session of council all canceled Choctaw warrants that may be found at the capitol building and elsewhere.

SEC. 2. That this resolution shall take effect and be in force from and after its passage and approval.

GREEN MCCURTAIN

Chairman Finance Committee.

Approved, Nov. 4, 1901. G. W. DUKES,

Principal Chief, C. N.

BILL NO. 26.

A RESOLUTION accepting the annual report of S. H. Woods, National Auditor for the fiscal year ended September 30, 1900

Your committee to whom was refe red the annual report of S. H. Woods, National Auditor, for the fiscal year ended September 30, 1900, have carefully examined the report, and find that Mr. Woods issued national warrants to the amount of $108.00 on certificates illegally issued by county and district clerks. For that reason, his report was not accepted by the General Council of October, 1900. Mr. Woods has collected the above amount from the parties who illegally issued the the certificates, and has submitted national warrants to your committee to the amount of $109.00

making a difference of one dollar in favor of Mr Woods, which amount your committee has refunded to him. The national Warrants thus turned in have been canceled by your committee

We would, therefore, respectfully recommend the adoption of the following resolution

Be it resolved by the General Council of the Choctaw Nation assembled :

SEC. 1. That the annual report of S. H. Woods, National Auditor for the fisical year ended September 30, 1900, be, and the same is hereby accepted as true and correct.

SEC. 2. That this resolution shall take effect and be in force from and after its passage and approval.

GREEN MCCURTAIN
Chm Finance Com.

Approved Nov., 4, 1901. G. W. DUKES,
Principal Chief, C. N

BILL NO. 27.

AN ACT Governing District Collectors.

Be it enacted by the General Council of the Choctaw Nation assembled:

SEC. 1 That there shall be appointed by the Principal Chief, by and with the advice and consent of the Senate, a collector for each one of three Districts of the Nation: Provided, That the present collectors shall hold office during good behavior and until October, 20, 1902. Each collector shall collect the tax on licensed traders and other persons or companies in his district; shall keep a correct account of the amount collected by him, and shall make a report at the end of each quarter to the Principal Chief and the National Treasurer, of the amounts collected by him, from each licensed trader and other person or company in his district during the quarter, for which the report is made.

Said report shall be made, on or before the twentieth day of the month, succeeding the last month of the quarter for which the report is made, and shall be accompanied by a statement sworn to before a notary or any other officer qualified to administer oaths.

Said statement shall be as follows: I .... collector of .... district, do solemnly swear that the accompanying report contains the true and correct amouuts collected by me from each licensed trader and other person or company in the .... district during the quarter commencing............190 and ending............190 and that the total thereof is the whole amount collected by me, which amount is enclosed herewith.

SEC. 2. *Be it furthar enacted*: That the first report under this act shall be for the quarter beginning October 1, 1901 and ending December 31, 1901, and shall be made as herein before provided. And that each collector shall also make an annual report to the General Council on or before the 10th day of October of each year, which report shall show the total amounts collected by him from each licensed trader and other person or company in his district during the fiscal year for which the report is made.

Said report shall be accompanied by a sworn statement similar to the one required for quarterly reports.

SEC. 3. *Be it further enacted*: That said collectors shall be entitled to receive for their services ten per centum of the amounts collected by them; and they are hereby authorized to retain ten per centum, but the remainder shall be sent by them to the National Treasurer with their quarterly reports: Provided however, That said collectors shall not be allowed to buy or speculate in National warrants. Any collector who shall buy national warrants or shall speculate in the same in any manner whatsoever shall be guilty of a felony and shall be indicted by the grand jury of his district and on conviction, such collector shall be fined not less than five hundred dollars, and upon his failure to pay the fine imposed he shall be imprisoned for one year in the district jail.

SEC. 4. *Be it further enacted:* That said collectors shall require all licensed traders and other persons or companies in their districts to furnish sworn statements of the amount of taxes paid by them, which statement shall be filed by the collectors with the National Treasurer with their quarterly reports.

SEC. 5. *Be it further enacted:* That said collectors are hereby authorized to deduct from the amount collected by them the fees charged for administering the oaths required by this act, not to exceed one dollar for each oath administered.

SEC. 6. *Be it further enacted:* That each appointee under this act shall be a citizen of the Choctaw Nation, and shall make bond, payable to the Principal Chief of the Choctaw Nation, in the penal sum of five thousand dollars, conditioned upon the faithful performance of all his duties, whfch bond shall be approved by the Principal Chief and filed in the office of the National Secretary. Said appointees shall each hold office for the term of two years: Provided however, that upon failure of any one of the collectors to comply with any and all of the provisions of this act, he shall be removed from office by the Principal Chief and his successor appointed, who shal hold office until the following council, when a collector shall be appointed accoading to section one, of this act: Provided further, that no collector shall be removed from office by the Principal Chief until he has been given an opportunity to answer any and all charges that may be preferred against him.

SEC, 7. *Be it further enacted:* That all acts or parts of acts coming in conflict with provisions of this act, are hereby repealed; and this act shall take effect and be in force from and after its passage and approval.

Passed the Senate Nov. 2, 1901. W. G. WARD,
Pres. Pro-tem of the Senate.

Pass the House, Nov. 2, 1901. WM. HARRISON,
Speaker of H. of R.

Approved, Nov. 4, 1901 G. W. DUKES,
Principal Chief, C. N.

White House, Washington, D. C., December, 3, 1901.
Approved: T. ROOSEVELT.

BILL NO. 28.

A RESOLUTION of adjournment.

Be it resolved by the General Council of the Choctaw Nation assembled:

That the present session of the General Council shall adjourn on Wednesday November 6, 1901 at 11. o'clock a. m.

Be it further resolved: That this resolution shall take effect and be in force from and aftar its passage and approval.

JAMES BOWER.

Approved Nov., 4, 1901

G. W. DUKES,
Principal Chief, C. N

BILL NO. 29.

AN ACT Amending the law relating to the Judicial Department.

Be it resolved by the General Council of the Choctrw Nation assembled:

That paragraph 1, section 3, page 130 Judicial Department, Durant's Code, Compilation of 1894, be amended so that it will read "In the Second Judicial District, on the first Monday of December and second Monday of July, at Sulphur Springs and shall be known and called Apuckshunubbee circuit court ground, instead of

"In the Second Judicial District, on the first Monday of December and July, at the Sulphur Springs, near the residence of Simion P. Williis, and shall be known and called Apuckshunubbee circuit court ground" and this act shall take effect and be in force from and after its passage and approval.

L. D. VAUGHN

Approved Nov., 29th 1901.

G. W. DUKES.
Principal Chief, C. N

BILL NO. 30.

AN ACT Authorizing the Circuit Judges to instruct the several county sheriffs to hold all persons charged with crimes felonies and misdemeanors who fail to give satisfactory bond.

Be it resolved by the General Council of the Choctaw Nation assembled:

SEC. 1. That the Circuit Judges of the three districts of the Choctaw Nation are hereby authorized and required to instruct the several county sheriffs in their districts to hold under custody all person or persons charged with crimes felonies and misdemeanors (except such as properly belong to the United States courts) who fail to give sufficient and satisfactory bond, and to hold said offender or offenders and board them from day to day and bring them to the circuit court for trial and keep them under custody until such case against such offender or offenders shall have been finally determined and disposed of and, the sheriff shall be allowed 50 cents per day for boarding of prisoners to be paid out of the couuty funds wherein the offense was committed.

SEC. 2. *Be it further enacted;* That all acts or parts or acts coming in conflict with this act shall be void, and that this act shall take effect and be in full force from and after its passage and approval. ROBERT BENTON.

Approved Nov. 4, 1901. G. W. DUKES,
Principal Chief, C. N.

BILL NO. 31

A RESOLUTION accepting the report of D. C. McCurtain delegate to Washington D. C.

We your committee to whom was referred the report of D. C. McCurtain delegate to Washington D. C., have given our careful consideration upon the same and find that said report is true and correct and that we would recommend the adoption of the following resolution:

Be it resolved by the General Council of the Choctaw Nation assembled:

That the report of D. C. McCurtain delegate to Washington D. C., be and the same is hereby accepted as true and correct.

Be it further resolved: That this resolution shall take effect and be in force from and after its passage and approval.

J. C. FOLSOM.

Approved Nov., 4, 1901.

G. W. DUKES,
Principal Chief C. N.

BILL No. 32.

A RESOLUTION Declining the petition of Williamson Mamby.

We your committee to whom was referred the petition of Williamson Mamby for the payment of a certain doctor bill claimed to have been paid by him for one Alvis Billy, who was sick with the small pox, have carefully considered said petition and are of the opinion that it should be denied.

We would therefore, recommend the adoption of the following resolution:

Be it resolved by the General Council of the Choctaw Nation assembled:

That the petition of Williamson Mamby for thirteen dollars claimed to have been been paid by him for one Alvis Billy who was sick with small pox be denied and this resolution shall take effect and be in force from and after its passage and approval.

JOE HOMER.
Chm. Com. on Petitions.

Approved Nov. 4, 1901.

G. W. DUKES,
Principal Chief. C. N.

BILL NO. 33.

AN ACT for the relief of Mrs. J. F. McCurtain.

Disapproved by the president Dec. 12, 1901.

BILL NO. 34.

AN ACT For the relief of Simpson Colbert.

Whereas, On the 24th, day of October 1900, one Simpson Colbert, Deputy Sheriff of Eagle County Choctaw Nation in discharging his duty as such officer, did pursue to arrest one Sim James for introducing whiskey in violation of the Choctaw laws; and said Sim James attempted to make his escape from the said Deputy Sheriff on a horse and was killed by running against a tree, and

Whereas, The said Simpson Colbert was arrested and a charge of murder and tried at Goodwater I. T. in the United States Commissioner's Court, and was released from said charge, and upon said arrest he was put to an expense of twenty-five dollars ($25.00) therefore,

We your committee to whom was referred the report of said Simpson Colbert, have found that he is entitled to the amount for which he asks, and we would therefore recommend the adoption of the following act.

Be it enacted by the General Council of the Choctaw Nation assembled:

SEC. 1. That the sum of twenty-five dollars ($25.00) be and the same is hereby appropriated out of any moneys in the National Treasury not otherwise appropriated for the relief of Simpson Colbert and that the National Auditor is hereby authorized and directed to issue his warrant in favor of said Simpson Colbert, and that the National Treasurer shall pay the same and this act shall take effect and be in force from and after its passage and approval.

Passed the Senate Oct 25, 1901.

GREEN MCCURTAIN,
President of the Senate.

Passed the House Oct. 25, 1901. WM. HARRISON
Speaker of the H. of R.

Approved Oct., 29, 1901. G. W. DUKES,
Principal Chief, C. N.

White House, Washington, D.C., December 2, 1901.
Approved T. ROOSEVELT.

BILL NO. 35.

We, you Finance Committee, who have had under consideration the matter of warrants issued by the National Auditor without authority of law, to Mansfield, McMurray & Cornish, have carefully considered the matter, and would respectfully report as follows:

SEC. 1. We find that the warrants were issued by the National Auditor on certificates duly signed by the Principal Chief. The warrants aggregate $7,596.40, and cover the salary and expenses of these partis from April 1, 1900, to and including July 31, 1901. Said warrants are as follows:

The following warrants are under head I, and were issued to Mansfield, McMurray & Cornish as salary account.

54	Feb. 13, 1901 Mansfield, McMurray & Cornish from April 1, 1900 to Jan., 31, 1901	$ 520.83
55	Feb 13, 1901 from April 1, 1900 to Jan 31, 1901	520.83
56	Feb 13 1901 from, April 1, 1900 to Jan 31 1901	520 83
65	Feb 13, 1901, from April 1, 1900 to Jan 31 1901	520 83
77	April 19 1901, from Feb 1, 1901 to Mar 31 1901	104 17
78	April 18 1901, from Feb 1, 1901 to Mar 31 1901	104 17
79	April 19, 1901, from Feb 1, 1901 to Mar 31 1901	104 17
80	April 19 1901, from Feb 1, 1901 to Mar 31 1901	104 17
102	Aug 24 1901, from Mar 31 1901 to July 31 1901	200 00
103	Aug 24 1901, from Mar 31 1901 to July 31 1901	200 00
104	Aug 24 1901, from Mar 31 1901 to July 31 1901	200 00
105	Aug 24 1901, from Mar 31 1901 to July 31 1901	200 00

Warrants issued to Mansfield McMurray & Cornish as expense account.

58	Feb 13, 1901, from April 1 1900 to Oct 29 1900	$1,547 95
81	April 1, " from Nov 1 1900 to Jan 31 1901	952 05
106	Aug 24 " , from Feb 1 " to July 31 "	1,513 10
107	Aug 24 " from Feb 1 " to July 31 "	250 00
	Total of expense account	$4,263 10

RECAPITULATION:

Salary Account	$ 3,333.30
Expense "	4,263.10
Grand Total	$7.596.40

The Principal Chief bases his authority for directing

the National Auditor to issue the foregoing warrants on an act approved by him October 29, 1900, entitled "an act for the payment of a certain contingent expenses necessary to protect the interests of the Nation, and increasing the contingent fund of the Principal Chief therefor." We invite attention to the fact that the act, above referred to was disapproved by the President of the United States, and that the Principal Chief therefore, had no right to direct the National Auditor to issue warrants thereunder for any purpose and that the National Auditor acted without authority of law when he issued said warrants.

SEC. 2 We find also, that, acting under the act, referred to above, the Principal Chief has allowed Mansfield, McMurray & Cornish a regular salary as general attorneys for the Choctaw Nation of $2,500.00 per year; their salary account has been rendered monthiy at the rate of $208.33 1-3 per month; that the Principal Chief has approved said accounts; and that the National Auditor has issued warrants thereon under instructions of the Principal Chief.

SEC. 3. We find further that Mansfield, McMurray & Cornish have been submitting accounts for the expenses claimed to have been incurred by them while representing the Choctaw Nation as general attorneys and citizenship attorneys; that these accounts have been approved by the Principal Chief; and that the National Auditor has issued warrants thereon.

We desire to state, however, that our investigation shows that Mansfield, McMurray & Cornish have performed services and incurred expenses in representing the Choctaw Nation in townsite and other matters, in tribal tax litigations and in various suits in which the nation was interested, and we believe that they should be allowed a reasonable compensation for the services performed and should be reimbursed for expenses actually incurred by them.

We have carefully examined the statements submitted by them to the Principal Chief purporting to be itemized accounts of services rendered and expenses incurred by them in behalf of the Choctaw Nation, but these statements do not contain information sufficient to justify the General Council in appropriating money in payment thereof. We believe that these parties should be required to submit to the General Council accounts showing in detail each item of expense incurred by them in each suit in which they appeared for the Choctaw Nation and that these statements should be accompanied by receipts from the parties to whom money was paid including the costs of printing briefs and of filing and docketing cases.

We believe also that these parties should not be allowed a regular salary, but should be allowed a reasonable fee for services actually performed by them, and that they should be required to submit accounts of such services.

We would therefore, recommend the adoption of the following resolution:

Be it resolved by the General Council of the Choctaw Nation assembled:

SEC. 1. That the Principal Chief be, and he is hereby authorized and directed to have Mansfield, McMurray & Cornish submit to the next General Council accounts showing the services performed by them and the different suits in which they appeared for the Choctaw Nation, from April 1, 1900, to and including July 31, 1901.

SEC. 2. That the Principal Chief be, and he is hereby authorized and directed to have Mansfield; McMurray & Cornish submit to the next General Council itemized statements showing each item of expense incurred by them in each suit in which they appeared for the Choctaw Nation, from April 1, 1900, to and including July 31, 1901.

SEC. 3. That the Principal Chief be, and he is hereby directed not to allow Mansfield, McMurray & Cornish a regular salary, but to allow them a reasonable fee for actual services when he deems it for the best interests of the Choctaw Nation to employ attorneys.

SEC. 4. That the Principal Chief be, and he is hereby authorized and directed to have Mansfield, McMurray & Cornish submit to the next General Council itemized statements and accounts showing the expenses incurred and the services performed by them in connection with each suit in which they may appear for the Choctaw Nation. after July 31, 1901.

GREEN MCCURTAIN
Chm Finance Com.

Passed over veto of Governer by two-third majority of both house.

SOLOMAN J, HOMER,
National Secretary,

BILL NO. 36.

A RESOLUTION rejecting the petition of Robert Benton.

We your committee to whom was referred the claim of Robert Benton to the amount of ($374.50) three Hundred and seventy-four dollars and fifty cents, have carefully examined said claim and find that said amount which he has asked is not justly due him and would recommend the adoption of the following resolution.

Be it resolved by the General Council of the Choctaw Nation assembled:

That the claim of Robert Benton for the amount of three hundred and seventy four dollars and fifty cents ($374.50) claim for malitia fees is hereby rejected.

HOUSTON NELON,

Approved Nov., 6, 1901.

G. W. DUKES,
Principal Chief C. N.

BILL No. 37.

A RESOLUTION Dissenting from the Statutory allowance of fifty doliars per mile as compensation for the right-of-way of the Gainesville, McAlester & St. Louis Railway company through the Choctaw and Chickasaw Nations under the act of Congress approved March 1, 1898.

(27 Stat. 524)

Be it resolved by the General Council of the Choctaw Nation assembled:

That the Choctaw Tribe of Indians hereby dissent from

the statutory allowance of fifty dollars per mile, fixed by section five of the Act of Congress approved March 1, 1893, granting the Gainesville, McAlester & St. Louis Railway Company a right-of-way through the Choctaw & Chickasaw Nations, upon payment therefor; and hereby certifies such dissent to the Secretary of the Interior.

Be it further resolved: That the Principal Chief of the Choctaw Nation is hereby authorized and directed to confer with the representative of the aforesaid railway company relative to the above dissent, and shall demand an amount that, in his judgement, may be deemed a just and proper payment, and ,his resolution shall take effect and be in force from and after its passage and approval.

J. C. FOLSOM.

Approved Nov. 6, 1901.

G. W. DUKES,
Principal Chief, C. N.

BILL NO. 38.

A RESOLUTION accepting the report of George W. Scott, National Treasurer.

We, your committee, to whom was referred the annual report of George W. Scott, National Treasurer, have carefully examined the same, and find that it covers the period from October 1, 1900, to and including September 30, 1901, and shows receipts and disbursements, os follows:

Total receipts	$ 96,220.95
Tótal Disbursements,	87,611.31
Balance on hand,	8,609.31

Your committee would, therefore, recommend the adoption of the following resolution.

Be it resolved by the General Council of the Choctaw Nation assembled:

SEC. 1. That the annual report of George W. Scott, National Treasurer, for the fisical year ended September 50, 1901, be and the same is hereby accepted as true and correct.

SEC. 2. That this resolution shall take effect and be in force from and after its passage and approval.

GREEN MCCURTAIN
Chairman Finance Committee.

Approved, Nov. 6, 1901.

G. W. DUKES,
Principal Chief, C. N.

BILL NO. 39.

GENERAL APPROPRIATION BILL

Be it enacted by the General Council of the Choctaw Nation assembled:

That the following sums of money are hereby appropriated out of the National Treasury to defray the regular and necessary expense of the government for the fiscal year commencing October 1, 1901, and ending September 30, 1902:

Principal Chief's salary	$2,000 00
National Secretary's salary	600 00
National Auditor's salary	600 00
National Treasurer's salary	600 00
National Attorney's salary	400 00
Private Secretary to Principal Chief, salary	1,000 00
Trustee, coal and asphalt under Atoka Agreement	4,000 00
National lighthorsemen,	1,400 00
Three supreme Judges,	1,200 00
Three circuit judges	1,500 00
Seventeen county judges	4,250 00
Three district chiefs	150 00
Three district attorneys	1,500 00
Election judges and Clerks	490 00
Grand and petit Jurors	7,050 00
Witnesses at circuit court	3,000 00
Contingent fund for National Auditor,	400 00
Contingent fund for Principal Chief	1,000 00
Contingent fund for National Treasurer	400 00
Contingent fund for National Secretary	450 00
Publication fund for " "	350 00
Sheriffs and deputies attending circuit courts	1,350 00
Clerk of supreme court	100 00
Three circuit clerks	900 00

Seventeen county clerks	1,700 00
Seventeen county Sheriffs	5,100 00
Thirty-four deputy sheriffs,	3,400 00
Seventeen county rangers	850 00
Sheriff attending supreme court	24 00
Superintendent of public schools	600 00
Contingent fund for Supt of public schools	450 00
Circuit and county judges pro tem.,	30 00
Act approved by Principal Chief, October 19 1899, and by President of the United States, January 10, 1900	5,000 00
Caring for capitol building,	75 00
Expenses of General Council	8,474 60
Citizenship commissioners and clerk,	7,200.00
Delegate to Washington, D. C.	2,500 00
To pay expenses of delegate to Washington, D. C.	1,000 00
Supreme Judges, mileage,	110 00
Three interpreters for circuit courts,	150 00

GREEN McCURTAIN,
Chairman of Finance Committee.

Approved Nov. 6th, 1901. G. W. DUKES,
Principal Chief, C. N.

BILL NO. 40.

The Finance Committee, in its examination of the annual report of S. H. Woods, National Auditor, for the fiscal year ended September 30, 1901, found that he had issued warrants on certificates of the district courts for the expens of interperters in the district courts to the amount of $56.50. Your committee believes that this expense should be borne by the Choctaw Nation, and that the present general council should make appropriation therefor.

Your committee would, therefore, recommend the adoption of the following act:

Be it enacted by the General Council of the Choctaw Nation assembled

SEC. 1. That the amount of $56.50 be, and the same is hereby, appropriated out of any money in the National Treasury not otherwise appropriated, to defray the expenses of interpreters in the three district courts during the fiscal year ended September 30 1901.

SEC. 2. That, inasmuch as the National Auditor has already issued warrants in payment of interpreters to the amount of 56.50, the General Council hereby declares legal all warrants issued by S. H. Woods, National Auditor, in payment of the following certificates:

No. 732 issued by James Culberson clerk of the first district for $16.00, not dated, in favor of Henry Sexton, interpreter; at the June special term, held June 11, 1901.

No. 582, issued by James Culberson, clerk of the first district, for $5, not dated in favor of Henry Sexton, interpreter, at the April special term, held May 2, 1901.

No, 18, issued by Simon Taylor clerk of the second district, for $20.50, dated July 8, 1901, in favor of Davis Noah interpreter, at the regular July term, 1901.

No- 50, issued by Will Everidge, clerk of the third district, for $15.00, dated February 9, 1901, in favor of Noah Peyton, interpreter at the February term, 1901.

SEC. 3. That this act shall take effect and be in force from and after fts passage and approval.

GREEN MCCURTAIN,
Chm. Finance Com.

Approved Nov. 6, 1901.

G. W. DUKES,
Principal Chief, C. N.

BILL NO. 41.

AN ACT to pay J. W. Ownby and A. P. Park for defending Jackson Billey et. al.

Not returned from the President.

BILL NO. 42.

AN ACT To provide for the payment of expenses of the removal of intruders and their property from the Choctaw Nation.

Not Returned from the President.

BILL NO. 43

AN ACT to relieve Drs. Le Roy Long and W. P. Hailey.

Your committee, to whom was referred the accounts of Drs. Le Roy Long and W. P. Hailey for services rendered in connection with the suppression of small pox in the Choctaw Nation, have carefully considered the accounts, and find that they each charge ten dollars per day for services rendered during the months of March, April and May, 1900 and that they have also render expense account as follows: Dr. Le Roy Long, $63.39, and Dr. W. P. Hailey, $64.37.

We find that the services were actually rendered, as set forth in the accounts, but we believe that eight dollars per day would be a reasonable compensation, and that they should not be allowed their expenses.

We would, therefore recommend the adoption of the following act:

Be it enacted by the General Council of the Choctaw Nation assembled:

SEC. 1. That the Principal Chief be, and he is hereby authorized and directed to pay Drs. Le Roy Long and W. P. Hailey the amount of six hundred dollars each for services rendered by them in connection with the suppression of small pox in the Choctaw Nation, out of the balance on hand of the ten thousand dollars appropriated at the session of October. 1900, to defray the expenses of the Board of Health.

SEE. 2. That the National Auditor shall issue a warrant in behalf of Drs. LeRoy Long and W. P. Hailey for the amount of six hundred dollars each on certificates of the Principal Chief and the National Treasurer shall pay the same.

SEC. 3. That this act shall take effect and be in force from and after ist passage and approval.

GREEN MCCURTAIN,
Chm. Finance Com.

Approved Nov., 6, 1901

G. W. DUKES,
Principal Chief, C. N.

BILL NO. 44.

A RESOLUTION Accepting the report of Hill and Brizzolara

We your committee to whom was referred the report of Hill and Brizzolara attorneys at law at Fort Smith Ark., in the case of the Choctaw Nation vs. Missouri, Kansas & Texas Railway Company, have carefully examined the same and find the same to be true and correct, and would recommend that your council adopt the following resolution:

Be it resolved by the General Council of the Choctaw Nation assembled:

That the report of Hill and Brizzalara be and the same is hereby accepted as true and correct. J. C. FOLSOM,

Approved Nov., 6th 1901. G. W. DUKES,

Principal Chief, C. N.

BILL NO. 45.

AN ACT Amending an act entitled an act creating a commission to accompany and assist the Dawes Commission making a roll of the Choctaw citizens and the amendment thereto.

Not returned from the President.

BILL NO. 46.

An ACT granting a charter to the Raymond Sans Bois Telephone Company.

Disapproved by the President.

BILL NO. 47.

A RESOLUTION Declining to accept the report of J. S. Forrest, Collector for First District of Choctaw Nation.

We, your committee, to whom was referred the report of J. S. Fourest, collector for the First District of the Choctaw Nation have carefully examined the report, and find that it covers the quarters ended September 30, 1900, December 31, 1900, March 31, 1901, June, 30, 1901, and September 30, 1901, and shows that the total amount due the

Choctaw Nation is $12,016.17. Your committee's examination of the report shows that the total amount due is $11,991.35.

Your committee was not furnished satisfactory evidence of the payment by Mr Forrest into the National Treasury of the amount due according to his report, or according to your committee's examination of the same, and we are advised by the National Treasurer that Mr. Forrrest has not turned into the National Treasury any moneys due the Choctaw Nation on royalties collected by him during the quarters named above.

Your committee would, therefore, recommend the adoption of the following resolution:

Be it resolved by the General Council of the Choctaw Nation assembled:

SEC. 1. That the report of J. S. Forrest, Collector for the first district of the Choctaw Nation, for the quarters ended September 30, 1900, December 31, 1900, March 31, 1901, June 30, 1901, and September 30, 1901, be, and the same is hereby, not accepted.

SEC. 2. *Be it further resolved:* That the National Treasurer be, and he is hereby authorized and directed to collect from J. S. Forrest, District Collector, the amount due Choctaw Nation according the the Finance Committee's examination of his report for the quarters named in section one of this resolution which amount is $11,991.35, and report his actions under this resolution to the next general council Provided, however, that upon refusal of J. S. Forrest, district collector, to pay the said $11,991.35, the National Treasurer is hereby authorized and directed to prosecute the said J. S. Forrest district collector, for embezzlment of public funds, and this resolution shall take effect and be in force from and after its passage and approval.

GREEN MCCURTAIN
Chm. Finance Com.

Operative by Constitutional Limitation.

Filed Nov. 14, 1901. S. J. HOMER,
National Secretary.

BILL NO. 48.

AN ACT amendatory to an act entitled "an act relating to the school system of the Choctaw nation.

Be it resolved by the General Council of the Choctaw Nation assembled:

That the act entitled "an act relating to the school system of the Choctaw Nation," approved October 30, 1890, be and the same is hereby amended so as to repeal all that portion and those provisions of said act which create and establish the office of school trustees for the several districts of the Choctaw Nation, and the office of district school trustees is hereby abolished.

SEC. 2. *Be it further enacted:* That the Superintenbent of public schools shall hereafter exercise, under the direction and supervision of the Principal Chief, the duties of the several district trustees, and, jointly with the Principal Chief, the functions of the Board of Education, as established and prescribed by said act of October 30, 1890. Provided, no duties contemplated by said act of October 30, 1890 to be done on the part of the district trustee, or the Board of Education necessary for the successful operation of our schools are hereby abrogated or curtailed, but the same may be performed by the Superintendent of Schools under the supervision of the Principal Chief as hereinbefore provided.

SEC. 2. *Be it further enacted:* That this act shall take effect and be in force from and after its passage and approval.

ROBERT BENTON,

Operative by Constitutional Limitation.

Filed, Nov. 14, 1901. S. J. HOMER,

National Secretary.

BILL NO. 49.

A RESOLUTION Refusing to accept the report of S. H. Woods National Auditor for the fiscal year ended Sept. 30, 1901,

Your committee, to whom was referred the anuual report of S. H. Woods, National Auditor, for the fiscal year ended September 30, 1901, have carefully examined the report and would respectfully report as follows.

SEC. 1. Mr. Woods has issued warrants, without authority of law on the certificates of district clerks, to the amount of $102.20.

SEC. 2. At the regular session of October, 1900, the General Council passed an act appropriating $500.00 for the relief of William H. Harrison. Immediately after the approval of the act by the Principal Chief, the National Auditor issued a warrant to Mr. Harrison as follows:

No. 8-I, for $500.00, dated October 12, 1900, and payable to Wm. Harrison, on account of "Act of council approved October 12, 1900.

Our investigation shows that the act, under which this warrant was issued, has not been approved by the President of the United States. Mr Woods should have waited until the act had been approved by the President of the United States before issuing a warrant thereunder. Your committee concludes that the above warrant was issned without authority of law and is therefore, illegal. The National Treasurer has refused to accept the warrant but we understand that the same has been cashed for Mr. Harrison by one of the District Collectors. Inasmuch as the warrant is illegal, and is yet outstanding, and inasmuch as Mr. Woods is liable to the Choctaw Nation for the amount of said warrant, we believe that Mr. Harrison should be required to reimburse the amount of the warrant to Mr. Woods.

SEC. 3. There was passed by the General Council at the regular session of October, 1900, an act entitled "An act for the payment of certain contingent expenses necessary to protect the interests of the nation, and increasing the contingent fund of the Principal Chief therefor." Under this act, the National Auditor issued warrants to the amount of $10,513.06, as follows:

To Mansfield, McMurray & Cornish, salary account.

54-I	Feb 13, '01	from April 1, 1900 to	Jan 31, '01	$ 520.83
55-I	"	"	"	520 83
56-I	"	"	"	520 83

57-I	"	"		"	520 83
77-I	Apr 19	Feb 1, 1901 to	Mar	"	104 17
78-I	"	"		"	104 17
79-I	"	"		"	104 17
80-I	"	"		"	104 17
102-I	Aug 24	Mar 31,	July	"	200 00
103-I	"	"		"	200 00
104-I	"	"		"	200 00
105-I	"	"		"	200 00

Total salary account $3,333.30

To Mansfield, McMurray & Cornish on expense account

58-I	Feb 13' '01	from April 1, '00 to	Oct 29, '00	$1,547 95
81-I	Apr 19,	Nov	Jan 31, '01	952 05
106-I	Aug 24,	Feb	July	1,513 10
107-I	"	"	"	250 00

Total expense account $4,263.10

D. W. Mulvane on expense account.

95-I	July 1, '01	March 31 '01	$ 417 66
96-I	"	June 30,	1,350 00
120-I	Oct	Sept	1,550.00

Total expense account $2,916,66

Inasmuch as the act, under which the foregoing warrants were issued to Mansfield, McMurray & Cornish and to D. W. Mulvane, was disapproved by the President of the United States, all warrants issued thereunder were issued without authority of law and are therefore illegal.

SEC. 4. Soon after the Supplementary Treaty had been signed on February 7, 1901, the Principal Chief, G. W. Dukes, went to Washington with a view of securing speedy action by congress on the treaty. For the expenses of that trip, he directed the National Auditor to issue two warrants of $1,000.00 each in favor of the Principal Chief, which $2,000.00 were deducted from the amovnt appropriated at the regular session of October, 1900, for the expense of the citizenship commission. Said warrants are as follows

56-I	February 15, 1901	G. W. Dukes	$1,000.00
59-I	"	"	1,000.00

Total, $2,000.00

Your committee believes that it was improper to charge the expenses of this trip to the citizenship Commission, and that the above two warrants were issued without authority of law, and are, therefore, illegal.

SEC. 5. In an act, approved by the President of the United States February 3, 1901, entitled "an act providing for a commission to treat with the United States Commission to the Five Civilized Tribes relative to closing the citizenship rolls, the amount of $200.00 was appropriated to meet all the expenses of the commission. The National Auditor has issued warrants under this act to the amount of $238.00, thus exceeding the appropriation by $38.00.

Your committee has already recommended to the present General Council that the Principal Chief be directed to require Mansfield, McMurray & Cornish and D. W. Mulvane to submit to the next general council itemized account of their services and expenses. When the next general council has that information, it may then consider the advisability of appropriating money to take up the warrants issued to the said Mansfield, McMurray and Cornish and D. W. Mulvane under the act entitled "an act for the payment of certain contingent expenses necessary to protect the interests of the Nation, and increasing the contingent fund of the Principal Chief therefor" referred to more particularly in paragraph 3, of this report; but, inasmuch as all of the foregoing warrants were issued without authority of law and are therefore, illegal, your committee believes that S. H. Woods, National Auditor, should be required to reimburse the National Treasury the following amounts:

Warrants illegally issued on certificates of district clerks,	$ 102.20
Warrant illegally issued to Wm H. Harrison,	500 00
Warrants illegally issued under the act entitled "an act for the payment of certain contingent expenses necessary to protect the interests of the nation, and increasing the contingent fund of the Principal Chief therefor,	$10,513 06
Warrants illegally issued to G. W. Dukes, Principal Chief,	2,000 00
Warrants issued in excess of amount appropriated to defray expenses of commission created under act approved February 3, 1901	38 00
Grand Total	$13,153 26

Your committee would therefore recommend the adoption of tde following resolution.

Be it resolved by the General Council of the Choctaw Nation assembled:

SEC. 1 That the annual report of S. H. Woods, National Auditor for the fiscal year ended Septembar 30, 1901, be, and the same is hereby not accepted.

SEC. 2 That the National Treasurer is hereby authorized and directed to make demand on the said S. H. Woods, National Auditor, for the amount of $13,153.26, and to make report of his actions under this resolution to the next general council.

SEC. 3. That this resolution shall take effect and in be force from and after its passage and approval

Passed over veto of the Principal Chief.

GREEN MCCURTAIN,
Chm Finance Comr

Vetoed by the Principal Chief and repassed by the House by two-thirds mafority Nov,, 6, 1901, and by the Senate Nov., 6, 1901. SOLOMAN J. HOMER,
National Secretary.

BILL NO. 50.

AN ACT Authorizing the sale of Spencer Academy and al the property belonging thereto.

Not returned from the President.

This is to Certify, That the above and foregoing is a full, true and correct copy of the Original Acts and Resolutions of the Choctaw General Council, passed at its Regular Session for the year 1901, the Originals whereof are now on file in the office of the National Secretary of said Nation.

In Testimony Whereof I, Solomon J. Homer, National Secretary of said Nation, have hereunto affixed my official signature and the seal of the Choctaw Nation. Done this the 15th day of Feb., in the year one thousand nine hundred and two.

SOLOMON J. HOMER,
[SEAL] *National Secretary, Choctaw Nation.*

INDEX